AFRICA TODAY AFRICA TODAY

African Landscapes

WARREN J. HALLIBURTON

EDITED BY

KATHILYN SOLOMON PROBOSZ

CRESTWOOD HOUSE
NEW YORK

MAXWELL MACMILLAN CANADA
TORONTO

MAXWELL MACMILLAN INTERNATIONAL
NEW YORK OXFORD SINGAPORE SYDNEY

AFRICA TODAY AFRICA TODAY

Dedicated to Mother Earth, and the generosity that supports the many families upon her.

Special thanks to Dr. J and Slo-Lo, Sandy, Barbara, Margaret, Rene, Lisa Joy, Morning Star, Gilbert, Michael (for making allowances) and, of course, PP. — KSP

ACKNOWLEDGMENTS

All photos courtesy of Magnum Photos.

Special thanks to Laura Straus for her assistance in putting this project together.

PHOTO CREDITS: COVER: *George Rodger; Inge Morath 4, 15; Burt Glinn 7, 36, 39; Chris Steele-Perkins 8, 27, 42; Eve Arnold 10; Marilyn Silverstone 13; Marc Riboud 16; Thomas Hoepker 18, 21, 23; Steve McCurry 29; George Rodger 31; Bruno Barbey 32, 35; Ian Berry 44*

Cover design, text design and production: William E. Frost Associates Ltd.

Library of Congress Cataloging-in-Publication Data

Halliburton, Warren J.
    African landscapes / by Warren J. Halliburton: edited by Kathilyn Solomon Probosz. — 1st ed.
    p. cm. — (Africa today)
    Summary: Introduces the African landscape, its rain forests, deserts, rivers and lakes, mountains, grasslands, and rifts.
    ISBN 0-89686-673-4
    1. Physical geography—Africa—Juvenile literature. [1. Africa—Geography.] I. Probosz, Kathilyn Solomon. II. Title. III. Series: Halliburton, Warren J. Africa today.
    GB330.H35 1993
    916'.02—dc20   92-37639

CRESTWOOD HOUSE
MACMILLAN PUBLISHING COMPANY
866 Third Avenue
New York, NY 10022

MAXWELL MACMILLAN CANADA, INC.
1200 Eglinton Avenue East
Suite 200
Don Mills, Ontario M3C 3N1

Macmillan Publishing Company is part of the Maxwell Communication Group of Companies.
First edition
Printed in the United States of America

1   2   3   4   5   6   7   8   9   10

Contents

Introduction

I f you were on a spaceship looking down at the earth, you would see a round blue ball with brown patches. The dark patches are land masses, known as **continents**. The deep-blue color is the water surrounding them. Water makes up 75 percent of the earth.

As your spaceship flew over the **equator**, you would see one brownish land mass that resembles an ice-cream cone with a slightly melted scoop of ice cream on the top. This is the continent of Africa. It is called the cradle of civilization, for it is here that the earliest signs of human life have been uncovered.

Africa is called the "**plateau** continent" because it has a much higher **elevation** that most other land masses. The plateau was created by massive outpourings of lava millions of years ago.

Africa is the second-largest continent after Asia. It is 5,000 miles long and 4,600 miles wide, with a total area of 11.7 million square miles. To the east it is bordered by the Indian Ocean, to the west, by the Atlantic Ocean.

Running through the very heart of Africa is the equator. The equator is an imaginary line, threading around the center of the earth, that receives the most intense sunlight. Because of its closeness to the equator, Africa has warm temperatures year round, through both the dry and rainy seasons.

On either side of the equatorial belt are hot, steaming jungles called rain forests. Rain forests make up just under 10 percent of the African landscape. They are called rain forests because of their climate, which is very, very wet. Plants and trees thrive in the humidity. In fact, the rain forests contain the most abundant plant and animal life of any place on earth.

Beyond the rain forests of Africa is desert. Desert and semidesert account for more than half of Africa's landscape. And Africa's deserts are among the driest places on earth. In the north of Africa is the world's largest desert, the Sahara. To the southwest are the Kalahari and Namib deserts. The deserts contain similar terrain: bare rock and towering rock formations, their shapes sculpted by the wind and gravel, sand dunes and oases.

But Africa isn't only desert and rain forest. Within its borders are "oceans" of grass. Africa contains millions of acres of **savannas**, or grasslands. The savannas, with grasses as high as a person's head, contain soil that is hard, coarse and reddish in color. The grasslands are dry, with soil too poor to support agriculture, but they are the favorite habitat of many animals. Grass eaters such as wildebeest, antelope, gazelle and zebra thrive in the savannas, and so do their predators — lions, cheetahs and hyenas.

There are many mountains in Africa, including Mount Kilimanjaro, the continent's highest mountain. Kilimanjaro is located almost at the equator, yet its peaks are covered with snow. Its lower slopes, though, are full of lush, green plants and tall trees.

And then there is the mist-covered Lengai Volcano, known as the Mountain of God. Its ashy gray slopes and treeless landscape are evidence of its last eruption in 1967.

The plateau of Africa contains many **upswellings**, ridges and **basins**, making travel across the interior difficult. As the plateau nears the coast, it slopes steeply into a narrow strip of lush plains. Bordering

the entire continent, this land has a warm, gentle climate, which allows for productive agriculture.

Rivers, with waters full of crocodiles, fish, hippos, and snakes, crisscross Africa. The Nile of Africa is the world's longest river. It is along its ancient banks that some of the earliest-known civilizations developed. The Nile is used for transportation, and its plentiful waters are used by farmers to irrigate their fields, allowing millions of people to survive. Scattered through Africa are the other life-sustaining rivers, including the Niger, Volta, Zambezi and Zaire.

In a low-lying depression of East Africa is the world's second-largest body of fresh water, Lake Victoria, which covers 26,828 square miles. More than 200 species of fish live in this lake.

Just to Lake Victoria's east are a series of shallow, **alkaline**, or salty, lakes. To Lake Victoria's west are a series of lakes thousands of feet deep that run in a chain through East Africa. All of these lakes were created by the African Rift System.

The African Rift System is one of earth's most amazing features. It is a series of **rifts**, or divides deep in the earth's crust, that have been ripping East Africa apart for millions of years. As the dividing took place below the earth, the surface was stretched, twisted, pushed up, and broken, creating some of the most spectacular landscapes on earth. The valley of the rift has steep sides and is gravelike in appearance.

Running 3,500 miles from Mozambique through the Red Sea, the African Rift System has two branches, an east and a west. They affect the land of a dozen nations. Not only was the rifting responsible for the creation of the deep lakes in the West Rift and the shallow, alkaline lakes of the East Rift, but it also created the volcanic mountains lining it.

Africa has always been called a land of mystery, and those who have been lucky enough to travel to this continent have come away full of respect for the land. This book will take you to some of the most spectacular features within the African landscape.

Rivers of Africa

The Nile River begins as a tiny trickle of water no bigger than a drip in your faucet. Yet, at 4,187 miles, it is the world's longest river.

The Nile winds through mountains, swamps, grasslands, tropical forests and desert before finally emptying into the Mediterranean Sea. Water buffalo, all kinds of birds, lions, antelope and other animals lap water and feed at its lush, green banks. Crocodiles lie just below the river's surface, waiting for unsuspecting turtles or other creatures to cross their paths. They eat whatever they can.

The sources of the Nile are deep in the heart of Africa. The southernmost source is a little spring on a hill in Burundi. Another is at Jinja, Uganda, on the fertile banks of Lake Victoria's north shore. Yet another source begins as ice at the tops of the six peaks of the Ruwenzori

Mountains in Uganda. The Ruwenzori are called the Mountains of the Moon because of their craterlike appearance.

The earliest recorded search for the Nile's source was in 460 B.C. by a historian named Herodotus. He traveled through thousands of miles of wilderness before turning back, giving up on ever finding the source of this rich river. It would take over 2,000 years and countless other searches, many of which cost explorers their lives, before the Nile's sources were finally found.

The Nile has two main branches. The first is called the Blue Nile, which runs for 1,080 miles. The second is the 2,285-mile-long White Nile.

Flowing north from Jinja, the White Nile (also called Victoria Nile at this point) crashes 130 feet down through Kabalega Falls into Lake Albert. It sips from many deep lakes, then flows into the Sudd, where it becomes more swamp than river.

The Sudd runs hundreds of miles and is as narrow as 40 to 50 yards at some points. It is clogged with papyrus reeds, which resemble long grasses, and hyacinth flowers, and has 15-foot-high walls of green vegetation on its banks. All kinds of birds skim the Sudd for insects and fish.

The Blue Nile begins at Lake Tana in the Ethiopian Highlands, about 6,000 feet above sea level. It cuts a huge swath through the Ethiopian plateau as it flows down. In some places, the river cuts a gorge one mile deep and 15 miles wide. No one travels down the Blue Nile — it is too dangerous.

The two rivers merge at Khartoum, Sudan, in what is known as the "longest kiss in history" to become the Nile. When they meet, the Blue Nile has much more force and has traveled a much shorter distance than the White Nile. It is the Blue Nile's waters that used to cause the Nile's yearly flood. About 85 percent of the total volume of water of the Nile comes from the Blue Nile.

After Khartoum, the Nile flows as a thin blue ribbon another 1,800 miles through Egypt to the Mediterranean Sea, at the northern end of Africa. Those entire 1,800 miles are through the fiercest desert in the world, the Sahara.

It is the Nile River that makes Egypt so different from the rest of Africa. The river transforms the dry desert on either side of it into a fertile area called the Nile Delta. The land surrounding the Nile has been farmed for thousands of years and served as the setting for one of the world's first great civilizations. It is for this reason that this area is called a cradle of civilization.

It is on the banks of the Nile that the great pyramids were built. The first was built for King Zoser around 2650 B.C.—almost 5,000 years ago! Today, the ruins of the 35 major pyramids are still standing. Many were discovered with their treasures inside. They are providing answers to scientists about how the ancient Egyptians lived.

The rich Nile Delta is dotted with rows and rows of farmers' crops. The squares of green end at the very edge of the desert. The farmers live behind the fields, in houses made of mud brick and Egyptian clover.

Every year the Nile used to flood this fertile river valley and cover the fields with water. When the waters receded, they would leave behind 20 million tons of rich soil, **silt** from the river as it made its voyage to the sea. This constantly replenished the soil nutrients that the plants and trees had used up as they grew.

In 1964 all that changed. The Egyptian government built a tremendous dam, the Aswan High Dam, nearly 600 miles upriver from Cairo, Egypt. The purpose was to control the annual flooding of the Nile and to harness the river for **hydroelectric** purposes. The High Dam is 364 feet high and 12,565 feet long, totally shutting off the Nile.

The waters of the Nile are diverted into Lake Nasser, one of the largest artificial lakes in the world. The 500-kilometer lake holds the equivalent of two years' worth of Nile water.

Farmers use this water source to irrigate their farms. Thanks to the High Dam, Egypt has been spared from several floods and periods of drought that gripped its neighbors. Now people can plant three crops per year instead of one.

But critics of the High Dam say that it has blocked the nutrient-rich silt that used to come with the yearly floods, thus making the land less fertile. Another problem that has arisen is that the land is much more **saline**, or salty. Many farmers say that the land is much poorer,

that they now need to use expensive **fertilizer** and that their harvests are not as great as in the time before High Dam.

One thing is clear, though. The Nile River is so life-giving that 96 percent of the population of Egypt lives within five miles of either side of it. The rest of Egypt is desert.

Another interesting African river is the Okavango. It begins as a stream swollen with rains from Angola's highlands, flows through Namibia, then into Botswana, and finally dies in the sands of the Kalahari Desert. Before it dies, however, it gives birth to the world's largest inland freshwater **delta**, the Okavango Delta. The Okavango Delta is also called the Jewel of the Kalahari. During the wet season, from May to October, the river forms a huge sheet of water a few feet deep that spreads across the burning desert sands to create a lush **oasis**.

During the wet season, antelope, zebra, rhinos, black egrets, storks, the largest herds of elephants in the world and other creatures migrate to the delta and have a feast.

Another important African river, the Niger of West Africa, flows in a 2,600-mile semicircle and empties into the Gulf of Guinea. Millions of West Africans depend upon it for their daily lives. They call it the river of hope, and the river of sorrow, for when it flows with abundance, it brings joy to the people. During times of drought, it brings sadness. *Griots*, or storytellers, share stories of the powerful and wealthy ancient empires that flourished in this area, such as the Empire of Mali. Thanks to the Niger, this area also contains some of the world's largest inland fisheries.

The Zaire River, once called the Congo, is nestled in the Congo Basin and flows through the rain forest. Hundreds of tributaries flow into this 2,700-mile-long river. They feed in 10 million gallons a second, making the Zaire the most powerful river in the world, after the Amazon.

The Zambezi River is unique for a different reason. Halfway between its mouth and its source is Victoria Falls. Here the river drops into a deep, narrow chasm, creating a canyon about 40 miles long. The mist and spray of the falls can be seen for miles. Its clouds and constant roar are described by the local people as smoke that thunders. It is so powerful that it produces a mini-rain forest.

The life-giving rivers of Africa provide the means for millions of Africans to survive. Without them, Africa would be a very sorry place indeed.

Deserts of Africa

I n the Sahara, the most reliable form of transportation is the camel. That is because cars can easily overheat in the more than 100-degree temperatures. Camels, though, can go for 12 days without water. Cars get stuck in the sand, but camels, with webbing between their two toes, amble along on the surface. During sandstorms the engines of cars get clogged with sand, while camels simply close their nostrils and keep moving.

The Sahara is the world's largest desert and makes up 59 percent of the African landscape. The United States could fit inside its borders with lots of room left over. Because it is so inhospitable, though, fewer than 3 million of Africa's 508 million people live within its borders. The desert dwellers are mostly **nomads**, herders who move from place to place, depending upon where they can find grass for their sheep, goats or cattle.

The Sahara fills Africa's northern third. It is 3,100 miles in length, running from the Atlantic Ocean to the Red Sea. Only the Atlas Mountains and Mediterranean Sea stop it from going further north. It runs south 1,200 miles into a semiarid region known as the Sahel. With each year, more Sahel land becomes desert.

The Sahara is called a weather desert since its dryness is caused by the atmosphere. The equator runs through Africa south of the Sahara. Hot air rises from the equator, cools, and forms rainstorms along this line. But at the surface of the desert, the rising air takes in the hot north-Saharan winds, which contain no moisture, so no rain can fall.

As is the case with the rest of Africa, the desert has two seasons, a wet and a dry. But you can hardly call the less than three inches of rain that falls mostly during June and October a wet season. In some places it doesn't rain for generations.

Rainwater evaporates before it soaks into the cracked earth. When there is a major downpour, dry riverbeds, or wadis, spring to life as the waters rush from the highlands, sweeping away everything in their path.

Truly, in the Saharan sands, you can fry an egg in the sand. The hottest temperature ever recorded was 136 degrees, in Al Azizia, Libya. Even in winter the temperature hovers around 100 degrees during the day. On winter nights, though, the air drops to freezing. Temperatures can vary by 100 degrees, and this sudden change causes rocks to split. And of approximately 4,400 hours of annual daylight, some 3,978 hours are direct sun.

In all, only one-fifth of the desert is sand. The rest of the landscape contains mountains; towering rock formations sculpted into strange shapes by the wind; high plateaus; flat, gravelly plains; salt flats and oases — the hearts that keep the Sahara alive.

The sand of the desert is all that is left of the rocks that have been blasted by the sun and wind over thousands of years. The wind blows grains of sand into great piles, called dunes, of all shapes. It is rightfully called the world's most creative sculptor.

Travel through the dunes is difficult. With each step, a person sinks up to the ankles in sand. No trees grow because the roots have nothing but particles of sand to grasp.

Dunes can be hundreds of feet high and roll on for hundreds of miles. When wind blows from the same direction onto the dunes, they form ridges, like waves on the sea. The front of the dune continually avalanches, causing the dune to slowly advance across the desert. These hills of sand are called live dunes. In areas with live dunes, it is easier to get lost than anywhere else in the desert.

The Qattara Depression, at 436 feet below sea level, presents a more deadly challenge. While its rippling pink, yellow, brown, red, blue and gold sands are breathtaking, it is always avoided. It is full of quicksand, and few survive its crossing.

There are two central mountain ranges in the Sahara. The first is in southern Algeria and is called the Ahaggar Mountains. The tallest peak is 9,852 feet high. The second range is the Tibesti Mountains in northern Chad, and they are 11,204 feet high at their tallest.

Hidden within these mountains are canyon pools. Today the nomads of the Sahara use this water for drinking and cleaning. Not so very long ago, their ancestors used these mountain areas as bases for raids on unwanted intruders into their domain.

The rest of the Sahara is made up of high, flat plateaus and low hills covered mostly with black gravel and rock.

The nomads know the Sahara the best. They can navigate through hundreds of miles of desert by the stars, or simply by small changes in the landscape. The ancient trade routes of the camel caravans that used to cross the desert have become the main roads crisscrossing the Sahara. But highway, in the Sahara, means a one-lane road. The Trans-Saharan Highway, the main route from the north to the south, is often "washed out" by sand. As cars search for an area where they won't sink into sand, the road grows wider and wider — up to 20 miles! Abandoned vehicles tell the story of travelers who became stuck and tried to walk to safety.

Far beneath the desert surface are great stores of underground water trapped in rock strata. These pools are called **aquifers**, and many governments hope to bring that water to the surface and turn the desert green. However, they must first drill from 300 to 6,000 feet down to get at it, which is very expensive and difficult. Yet aquifers have been tapped in Libya and other areas, bringing to the surface water that has been trapped underground for more than 5,000 years.

The areas where water bubbles up to the surface to create a patch of green are called oases. Oases support all kinds of wildlife, and their fertile soil grows date palms, vegetables, fruits and grains. Some oases are so small that they can only support one family. Others are large

enough to support entire towns. It is thought that the oases originally served as staging posts for nomads crossing the desert.

Today the date tree is the major resource of the oases. It is so important that the size of an oasis is measured by the number of date trees it has. One person can own the water rights to the tree, another the land, and several the date tree itself.

Houses must be swept every day because the wind blows tremendous amounts of sand into every corner. And just beyond the oases is the brown, parched earth of the desert.

In the open desert, wildlife exists, though not as plentiful as at the oases. Desert dwellers include mice, ants, flies, jackals, bats, lizards, vipers, long-legged spiders and scorpions. Butterflies and birds fly long distances across the worst terrain without stopping. Some insects live underground for years, waiting for rain to fall before they pop their heads up to the surface. Antelopes, mountain sheep, ostriches and foxes once were common, but now most have been killed by humans.

Strange as it may seem, the desert was once a fertile green land with many shallow lakes. Desert cave and rock pictures no more than 5,000 years old show two-wheeled chariots drawn by horses. Others depict buffalo hunts, people dancing, and hippos. The pictures were drawn by the people that lived in this area, and they could only have survived in a more moderate climate.

What happened is that the weather conditions in the Sahara gradually changed. The lakes evaporated, the grasses dried up and strong winds swept the topsoil away. This process is called **desertification**, the changing of grasslands into desert. All that is left of the fertile Sahara are its scattered oases — and the pictures left by our ancestors. One painting even shows a spindly cypress sapling. While the people who drew the tree are gone, the cypress tree lives on — right across from the painting. Judging from the rings of its trunk, it is between 2,000 and 3,000 years old!

The Namib and Kalahari deserts are located on the other side of the equatorial belt and are similar in makeup to the Sahara Desert. The Namib, though, has one unique difference. At night, fog rolls in from the Atlantic Ocean and condenses into droplets. Beetles and other insects come out at night and crawl to the tops of the dunes. They face the coast with their stomachs lifted high in the air. The droplets of water condense on their bodies, trickle down their legs and finally roll into their mouths.

The deserts can be deadly, but they are also beautiful. In the silence of the desert, people say, you can hear the voice of the soul. Those who live in the desert wouldn't trade this landscape for any other on earth.

The African Rift System

M illions of years ago a tremendous battle began. The battle-grounds stretched 3,500 miles, from Mozambique to the Red Sea. But it wasn't people who fought. It was a battle between the land masses of the earth itself.

And it happened deep below the surface of the earth, as the great, mobile plates, or rafts, upon which the continents rest began spreading apart in East Africa. As they spread, they violently wrenched apart the surface of the earth. These great cracks are called rifts. Each time the earth's crust shifted, earthquakes occurred. Ultrahot **magma** from below the plates shot through the gaps, creating a series of volcanoes that ran all the way from Tanzania to the northern tip of Africa.

This spreading apart occurred over millions of years and created the 3,500-mile African Rift System of central Africa. It is one of the most spectacular examples of the changing nature of landscape on the earth today. The rift has two branches, an east, called the Gregory Rift, after the Scottish explorer John W. Gregory, and a west.

The Gregory Rift runs south from Turkey; through Israel; along the Gulf of Aqaba; down the Red Sea; through the Ethiopian Highlands, Kenya and Tanzania; and into Malawi. It is traced by several shallow alkaline lakes and volcanoes.

The lakes of the Gregory Rift include Natron, Naduru, Bogoria and Elmenteita. Many are too hot to bathe in. But the minerals that can be extracted from them are valuable. At Lake Magadi the alkaline material called trona is refined to make glass and detergents; it is Kenya's number-one mineral export.

Humans cannot spend any length of time near some of these lakes because their skin can be burned and they can even be blinded by one of the alkalines, sodium carbonate. Most fish and wildlife avoid the alkaline lakes — except for the pink flamingo, which thrives on the lake bacteria and algae. More than half the world's population of pink flamingos live in the Gregory Rift.

The flamingos feed at Lake Naduru by the tens of thousands. When viewed from above, they look like massive clouds of pink against the dark-blue surface of the lakes. They nest in the muddy areas of a different lake, Natron. They dribble mud to build raised conical nests. The nests keep their eggs and chicks dry when the shallow water rises.

The Gregory Rift is flanked by Mount Kilimanjaro, Africa's highest peak at 19,340 feet. At its summit are three steaming volcanic craters, but it is dormant. Although Kilimanjaro is located almost at the equator, where it is very hot, its peaks are snow-covered.

Mount Kenya also lies along the rift and is even closer to the equator than Kilimanjaro. It too is a giant extinct volcano, but its rim has long since fallen away. What remains are the mountain's twin snow-covered peaks. Its misty slopes, though, are green-coated. Forests of bamboo; huge heather trees; giant, conical lobelia, which resembles cactus; ferns and other plants thrive on the mountainside. Long, beardlike lime-green mosses dangle from the branches of the heather trees, brushing against any mountain climbers.

Further south, at the Tanzanian border, is Lengai Volcano, which is still active. Lengai means "Mountain of God" in the Masai language. The mountain is almost all gray and is hollow. Its crust is so thin that a person's foot can break through the surface and be burned by the lava

flowing below. The top of the volcano is misted in clouds. Flowing down its steep sides are what look like ashy riverbeds — lava flows from the most recent eruption. Even the butterflies and birds fly quickly over this mountain toward the greener pastures below.

The Ethiopian Highlands created by the rift feed great rivers such as the Blue Nile. These highlands are much cooler and wetter than the surrounding lowlands. During times of normal rainfall, the Ethiopian Highlands are very fertile, and many farmers depend upon the land to make their living.

From the violence of the volcano, then, sprang one key benefit — fertility of the land. Wherever lava spilled over into the valleys alongside volcanoes, it created moist, rich soil, excellent for farming. Of course, it took millions of years for the rains to turn black rock into rich, red soil. Some of the most densely populated areas of Africa are in this region.

The rifting deep below the earth's surface never stops. A little more than ten years ago, 800 earthquakes shook the north end of the rift, near Lake Assal. Between the faults, rivers of red-hot lava miles long oozed to the surface. The faults caused the floor of the Red Sea to expand onto what used to be dry land. This is one of two sites in the world where scientists can actually observe a sea in the making.

The area surrounding Lake Assal is full of rocky black cliffs. Temperatures of 122 degrees in March are considered cool. The water of the lake evaporates rapidly, but is constantly replenished by the sea water bubbling up into it.

When the lake water evaporates, it leaves peculiar gifts behind — salt towers, salt sculptures and salt paintings along the shoreline. In the shallow waters, the salt looks like a fine sprinkling of snow. The nomads travel by camel from afar to mine the lake's salt.

The West Rift is different in nature from the Gregory in that it leaves a great chain of lakes thousands of feet deep in its wake. It runs through the heart of Africa, along the border of Zaire and its eastern neighbors, Uganda, Rwanda, Burundi and Tanzania. Lakes Albert, Edward, Kivu, Tanganyika, Rukwa and Malawi are included in this rift, and these are the waters from which the Nile River flows.

Between Lake Kivu and Lake Edward rise the eight volcanoes of the Virunga range. Two of these volcanoes are still active. The Virunga Mountains are almost always clouded over, very damp, emerald-green and full of wildlife. They are home to the endangered mountain gorilla.

Along the Virunga slopes farmers grow bananas, millet and vegetables. Most of the mountainside forests have been cut down and turned into farmland.

If the day is very clear, you can look down from the Virungas and see in the distance the shimmering blue waters of Lake Victoria, the world's second-largest freshwater lake. Lake Victoria, while not part of the African Rift System, lies in a depression between its two branches. North and east of the lake, peanut, cotton, sesame and corn fields blanket the horizon, along with herds of cattle.

Lake Victoria feeds the Victoria Nile, which crashes 130 feet down through Kabalega Falls into Lake Albert. To the south of Lakes Albert, Edward and Kivu is Lake Tanganyika, the world's longest freshwater lake. It is the oldest lake in the rift and is 420 miles wide and more than 4,700 feet deep! In some areas of the lake oil seeps to the surface, creating natural oil slicks. This fossil fuel could one day be tapped by the nations bordering the lake.

Within the deep lakes of the West Rift live aquatic cobras, fish and crocodiles. The lakes contain species of cichlids, tiny fish with neon colors — oranges, bright yellows, shiny purples and silvers — and designs not found anywhere else in the world.

While most of the mountains were created by volcanoes, some were created when the plates below the earth crushed together, forcing up the surface of the earth to create "fold mountains."

The Ruwenzori Range, or Mountains of the Moon, which runs on the Uganda-Zaire border, are fold mountains, as are the Atlas Mountains bordering the Sahara in north Africa. The Atlases are Africa's longest mountain range, running from Morocco to Tunisia.

It's not the Atlas Mountains, but the African Rift System that holds the most interest to many scientists. Throughout the system, the faulting and uplift of the earth has exposed lake and river sediment and volcanic ash and helped preserve fossils estimated to be 4 million years

old. These fossils are helping **anthropologists** and **archaeologists** solve the mystery of how human beings developed.

The bones of one of the earliest known ancestors of humans was discovered in the rift system at Hadar, Ethiopia, in 1974 by anthropologist Donald C. Johanson. Scientists named the fossil Lucy. Lucy is thought to have walked the earth 3 to 4 million years ago.

Scientists also study the fossils of Olduvai Gorge, a 25-mile canyon. The thousands of fossils collected are helping to piece together the story of how human beings developed.

Among the fossils found at Olduvai Gorge were long trails of footprints frozen in the volcanic ash. These were discovered by Mary Leakey in 1978. Preserved forever in lava, these footprints provide us with a link to our past, a past that began in the lands of Africa.

Tropical Forests of Africa

The rain forests of Africa flank either side of the equator, where the amount of sunshine and the length of the day is almost the same year round. This rain-forest belt includes the Congo Basin coastal area, eastern Madagascar (the world's fourth-largest island), the East African highlands and the mountains of the northwest.

The tropical rain forests of Africa, like other rain forests, contain the richest, most abundant growth of plant life anywhere in the world. This is not because of rich soil, but because of the recycling of nutrients from plants' fast decomposition.

People say that the rain forest has two climates: wet and wetter. And the jungles banding around the equator have been there for tens of millions of years.

One acre of jungle contains 100 different kinds of tall trees, including fruit, olive, oak, mangrove, ebony, mahogany and myrtle. It is simply impossible to compute the number of insects. The different species of birds number close to a thousand.

The floor of the forest is thin, hard and dark, with a thick mat of tree roots very close to the surface. Thick foliage and vines block out 95 percent of the light that falls on the tops of the trees. The air here is hot, stagnant and loaded with moisture, which causes plant matter to decompose very rapidly. For example, it takes an oak leaf in Europe one year to decompose, while a leaf that has fallen on the jungle floor decomposes in six weeks. Only those flowers that need very little light can grow here. Most of those found on the ground are dead, having fallen from the treetops.

Only a few animals live on the forest floor, including the okapi, a primitive giraffe, and the royal antelope, which is about the size of a hare. They live off nuts and fruits fallen from above. Others live off tubers and roots just below the surface. Termites thrive on the decomposing material, which they convert into living tissue. In turn, they support an enormous ant population, which raids the termite nests.

Most of the activity in the rain forest doesn't occur on the ground, though. It comes 150 feet above the ground, at the tops of the trees, in what is called the canopy. In the fresh air and sunshine of the canopy, most rain-forest creatures make their homes. The canopy, approximately six to seven yards deep, is a meadow of leaves and completely different from the ground.

At the very tops of the tallest trees, crowned eagles make their nests. Birds, small mammals, including bats known as flying foxes, and all kinds of insects live in the rest of the canopy. They are very well fed, for the fruits of the trees become ripe at different times of the year, giving the creatures a year-round feast. The community of animals wanders from tree to tree, plundering each as its fruit ripens. Monkeys become quite picky and sniff each fig on the fig trees individually to see if it is to their liking.

Each of the canopy's leaves is angled toward the sun to collect the maximum amount of light. The leaves are a glossy, waxy green color.

This waxy surface makes it difficult for moss and algae to take hold. The leaves also have drip tips, spikes at their ends that create rainspouts for the water to run off.

Bark and branches, though, aren't so lucky. They collect lots of moisture and lots of unwanted "guests." Masses of green algae coat the bark of trees and branches, dangling even from the tiniest of twigs. Jungle vines hang from the branches too. Mosses and ferns grow in the crevices of bark. As the trees get older, they support huge lines of ferns and orchids. These plants in turn have lodgers of their own: beetles and other insects.

The rain forest, while not an easy place for most humans to live, nonetheless contains in its flora and fauna the cures for many illnesses of humankind. In fact, most of the substances in most of the medicines we use today can be found in the rain forests. This is one reason why it is so important to preserve them.

The Serengeti Plain

It is sunset on the Serengeti Plain of East Africa. The tall yellow-and-green grasses are rustling, but there is no wind. The sound is ignored by the zebra, wildebeest and other animals drinking side by side at a swollen stream. The rustling sound comes closer, closest to a baby wildebeest lapping water alongside its mother. Then a wind rises, sweeping the grasses back — to reveal a lioness about to pounce.

The world stops as the animals and the predator eye one another. In the next instant warning cries burst from the lungs of the animals. They dash wildly away from the stream as the lioness leaps for the infant wildebeest. This time the baby is lucky. She escapes headlong through the grasses, racing after her mother.

The lioness gives chase, leaving the stream in the Serengeti silent and abandoned. Then the cries die down, the wind grows still and the sun continues to sink below the horizon of Africa. The day is ended on the Serengeti Plain.

Serengeti means "extended area" in Masai. Indeed, the Serengeti is an ocean of grass that runs through Tanzania and Kenya, just east of the Gregory Rift. This area is also called the savanna. The climate is dry, with a hard, coarse reddish soil that doesn't let many trees take root or crops grow. But these same features create a perfect environment for grasses to flourish, which has made the Serengeti a favorite home for more than one-quarter million grass-eating animals. The grasses grow back even when they are cropped low by grass eaters.

One square acre of savanna can support the weight of more living flesh than any other kind of country. Some of the last great animal herds on earth live in the Serengeti.

The Serengeti contains a tremendous variety of grasses, some growing higher than a person's head, and multicolored wildflowers flourish here. Rivers and streams, home to many rhinos, flow throughout the plains. Wherever there is a water hole, dozens of species of animals sip its waters. Great piles of boulders, called kopjes, which have trees growing on them, dot the landscape.

Scattered throughout the Serengeti and other grassland areas are trees whose roots have been able to penetrate the hard-packed soil, including acacias and thorny bushes, the branches of which giraffes especially love to eat. In the northern part of the Serengeti, where the land is wetter, there are woodlands.

Another tree that grows in the savannas — and throughout Africa — is the huge baobab tree. Baobabs soak up water in their bloated trunks. They serve as filling stations for creatures of the wild. While they seldom grow to more than 60 feet in height, mature trees have trunks that range from 30 to 50 feet in diameter! They can live to be more than 2,000 years old.

The baobab grows purple-and-white flowers and a fruit called monkey bread that dangles from its branches like hanging lanterns. The fruit holds many seeds. The pulp serves as food or flavoring for cool drinks. Many people use the leaves and bark in medicines. They also use the bark fibers to make paper, cloth and rope.

Nearly every acre of the Serengeti teems with animals. Those who live off the Serengeti grasses and trees include the zebra, impala, Thomson's gazelle, wildebeest and elephant. The animals know exactly which grass is sweetest and ready to be cropped. When it is eaten, they move on to the next island of grass.

Small creatures such as termites and ants help to crop the grasses of the Serengeti short too. The insects in turn are fed upon by anteaters, other insect eaters and birds. In a single day an adult giant anteater can eat 30,000 termites!

Small hunters such as weasels and jackals prey upon giant rats, spring hares and ground squirrels. The big **carnivores** such as lions, hunting dogs, cheetahs and hyenas in turn feed on them — and of course on the large grass eaters. Sometimes three lions will work

together to bring down one wildebeest. And many carnivores hide in the grasses just beyond the streams, waiting for unsuspecting animals to come for a drink.

Elephants have been coming in increasing amounts to the savannas. They like acacia and a few other trees — a little bit too much. They snap them off as if they were thin little sticks, sometimes leaving a trail of destruction miles long. They are helping to convert the Serengeti woodlands into grasslands. Elephants didn't live in this area until the 1960s, when human development began driving them out of their original homelands.

During the wet season, from December until May, the animals graze in the southeastern parts of the desert. By the end of May the area is at its driest, and the grass has been cropped low. It's time for the animals to migrate north. The wildebeest herds, which number up to 1.5 million animals, don't let any obstacle stop them. Their thundering hooves cross rivers and stampede down cliffs, kicking up dust clouds miles high.

Lions and other predators follow the migration, picking out the tired animals and downing them with lightning-quick speed.

Eventually the great herds reach the woodlands in the north. They stay until the rain begins to fall in November, at which point they start their journey back to the southern plains, and the cycle begins anew.

Landscapes and Humans

S o far we have discussed the landscape without much talk about humankind. It is necessary to say a few words about how Africa's nearly 700 million people get along with the land.

Because of the fact that 59 percent of the continent is desert or semiarid, this land cannot be used for farming, and very few people live in it. The rain forest, which accounts for a little less than 10 percent of Africa, is also not hospitable to most human beings.

Twenty percent of the continent is infected with the tsetse fly, which causes sleeping sickness in humans and diseases in cattle. People cannot live in infected areas. The savannas are too dry, with soil too poor, to support agriculture.

This leaves less than one quarter of Africa that is hospitable to most human life. And Africa has only two seasons, dry and wet, and it is very dependent upon the rains. But the rains do not come regularly. When there is a drought, it grows worse as you go north.

Seventy percent of the African people live off the land. Because of recent droughts, millions of people right now are suffering from lack of food.

The African plateau, with its ridges, steep slopes, and basins, has made it very difficult to develop transportation across the continent. Many of the rivers are too dangerous to travel upon. And there are 14 landlocked countries.

Most of the people on the African continent live in the areas where the soil is fertile, especially around the volcanoes in the African Rift System. In Uganda, Rwanda, Kenya and Zaire, the population is extremely dense. The Virunga Mountain slopes, where once the mountain gorillas roamed freely, have been almost totally denuded of trees.

The population of Africa is increasing dramatically. Too many people are attempting to make a living by farming. Each year thousands of acres succumb to the plow or to development for ranching. Forests are also being cut down because people use the trees for firewood, to build their homes and as fencing around their livestock.

In the Sahel, the semiarid area just south of the Sahara, the desert is expanding not because of the weather, but because the people are overfarming and overgrazing the land. Regeneration in some areas might take 20,000 years!

The elephants that used to range across central and south Africa are being forced out of their habitats, their migratory patterns interrupted by encroaching farmland. And farmers, to protect their crops, will shoot them. More and more are dying each year. The last great herds of elephants are now living in lands protected by the various governments of Africa.

Other Africans make their living by hunting. To prevent all the animals from being killed off, many of the 52 African countries have set aside enormous tracts of land for the animals to live. But **poachers**, or those who illegally kill animals, sneak in and kill the animals anyway.

Since 1600, 350 species in Africa have become extinct. It is difficult to stop all the poachers because many of the African reserves cover millions of acres. Most of the governments that created the parks don't have a lot of money, so they can't hire enough staff to keep the poachers out. Many poachers claim that they must kill the animals to provide food for their families. Truly, only in the Serengeti and in little-developed areas of Botswana do the plains animals run in the huge herds that were once common in Africa south of the Sahara.

People say that the challenge isn't to develop Africa, but to hold on to what is there already. Wise land-conservation efforts, along with more and more people joining the fight to preserve Africa's natural landscape, are helping to achieve this.

Today people are still free to climb the green, misty slopes of Mount Kenya. They can study the rain forest and still hear the chatter of the canopy creatures above them. They can explore the freedom of the vast, open, grassy Serengeti, sleeping under a night sky thick with stars. These remain the natural landscapes of Africa.

PHOTO IDENTIFICATION

(Cover) Mt. Kilimanjaro\Tanzania; (4) the bank of the Nile River\Egypt; (7) a water pool in the savannah\Kenya; (8) fishing on Lake Victoria\Kenya; (10) a sailboat on the Nile\Egypt; (13) the convergence of the Blue and White Niles\Egypt; (15) the Aswan High Dam monument\Egypt; (16) the Nile River\West Africa; (18) the Sahara Desert\Algeria; (21) sand dunes\Algeria; (23) an oasis\Algeria; (27) Uhuru peak, the highest point of Mt. Kilimanjaro\Tanzania; (29) the Atlas Mountains\Morocco; (31) hippos in Lake Edward\Uganda; (32) a bamboo forest\Gabon; (35) a canoe travels on a river through a forest\Gabon; (36) zebras on the Serengeti Plain\Tanzania; (39) lions\Tanzania; (42) Nairobi National Park\Kenya; (44) Table Mountain\South Africa

Glossary

Alkaline   Salty or acidic.

Anthropologist   A person who studies the history of human beings.

Aquifer   Underground pools that form when water is trapped between layers of rock.

Archaeologist   A person who studies the remains of past civilizations.

Basin   An area of the earth where the ground has sunk to form a depression.

Carnivore   An animal that eats meat.

Continent   One of the seven main bodies of land into which the globe is divided.

Delta   The mouth of a river.

Desertification   The process by which land is turned into desert through overgrazing or overuse.

Elevation   The distance in height something is from sea level.

Equator   The name for the imaginary line that circles the earth and divides it in half.

Fertilizer   Substances added to soil to provide nutrients that are not present naturally.

Hydroelectric   The process of creating electricity using the force of flowing water.

Magma   Molten rock found below the earth's surface.

Nomads   People who live in the deserts of Africa and travel from place to place with their herds.

Oasis   An area of lush vegetation surrounded by desert.

Plateau   A flat, elevated area of land.

Poacher   A person who hunts animals illegally.

Rift   Divides that form when the plates below the earth's surface shift and pull apart.

Saline   Containing salt.

Savanna   A dry, treeless plain or grassland.

Silt   Rich soil left behind when a river floods and then recedes.

Upswelling   An area of the earth where the ground has been pushed up to form a mound or ridge.

Index

MORE
SOUTHERN
STEAM IN THE WEST COUNTRY

TONY FAIRCLOUGH AND **ALAN WILLS**

D. BRADFORD BARTON LTD

Frontispiece The Wenford Bridge freight from Wadebridge is hauled, for the last time, by a Beattie well tank. No.30587 pulls its load across the road at Dunmere, heading towards its destination on 20 August 1962, the culmination of over sixty years of successful service by the Beatties on this mineral line. Note the shunting pole visible on the front of the engine.

[G. D. King]

 © *copyright D. Bradford Barton Ltd 1975*   *I S B N 085153 186 5*

printed in Great Britain by Thomson Litho Ltd, East Kilbride, Scotland

for the publisher

D. BRADFORD BARTON LTD · Trethellan House · Truro · Cornwall · England

introduction

Exeter has been a rail centre since 1 May 1844, when the lines from Bristol reached the West Country city. Its importance grew with the years, a further significant date being 19 July 1860, when the L S W R line via Salisbury provided an alternative and shorter route to the capital. The L S W R constructed a network of lines which converged on Exeter from Plymouth, North Devon and North Cornwall, while numerous branches served towns not fortunate enough to be on the through routes. Naturally there was rivalry with the Great Western, competition which provided an incentive for the L S W R—and its successors, the Southern Railway and Southern Region—to maintain an efficient and useful service for the inhabitants of the West Country. These Southern lines suffered severely under the Beeching plans of 1963; many are closed, the track beds lost beneath a carpet of wild vegetation, bridges are blown, stations derelict or sold as dwellings. And now, a decade later, the West Country roads are choked with queues of cars and the rural peace is shattered by heavily laden lorries thundering along narrow, twisting country roads. Already there are rumblings of regret that the railways have been so drastically pruned.

This volume depicts further scenes along the various Southern routes radiating from Exeter and the editors hope it will keep fresh the memory of those engines which seemed so much a part of the West Country—the 'King Arthurs' and Drummond tanks, the 'Merchant Navies' and 'Woolworths', the 'T9s' and above all, our own special locomotives, the 'West Country' Pacifics. They fitted so well into the verdant background of this part of Britain—and now they are gone.

The summer of 1946 brought peace-time working back to railways in the West Country. Holiday reliefs carried war-weary passengers in vast numbers to and from London and the coastal resorts of Devon and Cornwall. Fortunately the early teething troubles of the Bulleid Pacifics had by this date been largely overcome, enabling these powerful machines to take a full share in this intensive traffic. The doyen of the 'Merchant Navy' Class, No.21C1 *Channel Packet*, with steam sanders working, leaves Exeter (Central) with the 12.55 p.m. for Waterloo on 26 August. Only this engine and its sister No.21C2 had the cast brass number plates and 'Southern' tender plates when built at Eastleigh in 1941.

[Brian A. Butt]

The Southern built a large locomotive depot at Exmouth Junction on the eastern outskirts of the city. In its heyday one hundred engines were maintained here, including a large allocation of Bulleid Pacifics for express passenger turns. By March 1965, when this view was taken the shed had become the home of numerous Standard and ex-GWR locomotives as well as the remaining SR types left in the West Country. Class '3' 2-6-2Ts Nos. 82040 and 82042 are being prepared for duty with 4-6-2 No. 34048 *Crediton* prominent in the foreground.   [J. R. Besley]

Although the engine livery is BR lined black, this scene at St. James's Park Halt, half a mile east of Exeter (Central) April 1953, is reminiscent of LSWR days, as Drummond 0-4-4T No.30667, built in 1897 heads towards Exmouth with train composed of LSWR non-corridor stock.

[P. J. Lyn

The Standard Class '4' 2-6-4 tanks were late arrivals in the West of England, where they proved to be popular replacements for the veteran Drummond tanks. Closely based on the highly successful Stanier and Fairburn designs for the LMS, these fast and powerful engines operated from Exmouth Junction shed in the early 1960's, having been made redundant in the Central Section area. No.80038 storms away from Polsloe Bridge Halt, near Exmouth Junction, with the 2.15 p.m. from Exeter on 26 January 1963.

[W. L. Underhay]

Post-war Ivatt Class '2' No. 41306 runs down the 1 in 50 bank into the station at Budleigh Salterton with an Exmouth to Tipton St. John's branch train on 29 August 1958. This train will connect with the Sidmouth line trains at Tipton. [G. D. King]

A down express approaches Sidmouth Junction on 16 August 1958 hauled by one of the popular 'King Arthur' 4-6-0s, No.30784 *Sir Nerovens*. This engine was one of thirty built in 1925 by the North British Locomotive Company of Glasgow and known as 'Scotsmen' by the engine crews who handled them.

[G. D. King]

'Next stop Broad Clyst!' Exmouth Junction Pacific No.34023 *Blackmore Vale* steams out of Pinhoe, three miles out from Exeter with the 1.10 p.m. Exeter to Salisbury on 14 December 1963. The simple wooden signal box is of typical LSWR design for small stations.

[W. L. Underhay]

The Eastleigh-built 'Arthurs' of 1925 could be distinguished by the LSWR type of cab which contrasts with the Maunsell design illustrated above. No. 30448 *Sir Tristram*, of Salisbury shed, races downgrade near Honiton in the late 1950's.

[Brian A. Butt]

No. 30023 calls at Tipton St. John's on its 8¼ mile journey from Sidmouth Junction (now named Feniton) to Sidmouth in April 1954.   [J. R. Besley]

Drummond 'M7' 0-4-4T No.30676 pulls away from Sidmouth with Bulleid coaches to be attached at the Junction to a Waterloo-bound express on 20 August 1958. The branch was opened to Sidmouth in 1874, providing a local service to Exeter and through coaches to Waterloo until the Beeching Axe fell. [G. D. King]

Old stock and modern motive power are combined on 20 August 1958 as the branch train, composed of L S W R and S R coaches nears Sidmouth behind Standard Class '3' 2-6-2T No.82023. Although the Drummond tanks were well liked, the greater comfort of the cabs of the modern Standards was much appreciated by the men who handled them during the final decade of steam working in the West. The branch was closed in March 1967. [G. D. King]

Standard Class '3' No. 82023 pounds up the 1 in 40 past Harpford Woods, near Tipton St. John's, with its train for Sidmouth on 2 September 1955.
[G. D. King]

With eighteen miles of downhill running ahead, the fireman of No. 35026 *Lamport and Holt Line* will be relaxing on the footplate as the 11.0 a.m. Waterloo to Ilfracombe express, having cleared the summit of the gruelling climb of Honiton bank, bursts out of Honiton Tunnel on 27 June 1964.
[W. L. Underhay]

A Templecombe to Exeter local pulls away from Seaton Junction in July 1958 behind versatile 'S15' No. 30827, of Salisbury (72B) shed. These Maunsell-designed 4-6-0s, with 5ft 7in driving wheels, were a mixed-traffic version of the 'King Arthurs' and acted as the principal heavy goods engines on the West of England route, but took their turn at handling a variety of passenger duties when the need arose. Fifteen members of the class were built at Eastleigh in 1927, followed by a further ten in 1936.

[Derek Cross]

A goods rattles past Seaton Junction on the up through road in September 1959 with 'S15' No. 30846 at its head. The long descent of Honiton bank has enabled the fireman to have a breather and allowed the engine's boiler pressure to pull around after the pounding climb up to the tunnel from Honiton. The homely appearance of the LSWR signal box serves as a reminder of the faithful work performed by countless numbers of signalmen before electronics and automation rendered many of these boxes redundant.

[Derek Cross]

The classic scene on the Seaton branch; motor-fitted Drummond 'M7' 0-4-4T No. 30045 propels its two-coach train of SR stock on the 4½ mile run to Seaton in July 1958. The air pump for the 'push and pull' apparatus is visible on the locomotive's smokebox, while for identification purposes, the train's tail lamp is carried on the centre of the buffer beam.

[Derek Cross]

The 1960's saw many 'Farewell to Steam' tours throughout the South and West; Ivatt tanks Nos. 41206 and 41308 stand in Seaton Junction station while the tourists survey the nostalgic scene. [John H. Meredith]

Following the Western Region's take-over of all lines west of Salisbury in 1963, ex-GWR engines appeared on old Southern territory. Pioneer pannier tank No. 6400 approaches Seaton Junction with the 3.47 p.m. from Seaton on 22 June 1963. All traffic ceased in March 1966.

[W. L. Underhay]

Another Western type to put in an appearance was the Collett 14xx 0-4-2T. No. 1450 is seen leaving Colyton on the 2.3 p.m. to Seaton on 10 March 1965. [W. L. Underhay]

No. 30582 makes a dignified entrance into Combpyne platform on 13 August 1960. The camping coach was one of the once popular amenities provided by the railways for holiday makers in the West Country.   [P. J. Lynch]

The 6¾ mile Lyme Regis branch, which joined the main line at Axminster, was always of special interest to railway buffs, for this was the domain of the Adams 4-4-2 tanks. In this view at Axminster, the 'Grand Old Lady' of the line moves off with through coaches from London in September 1959. First appearing for trials in 1913, No. 30582 (ex-L S W R No. 0125) remained on the branch until final withdrawal in 1961. Two other 'Radial Tanks', Nos. 30583–4 survived to be taken into B R stock.   [G. D. King]

No. 30582 again, this time backing on to its train at Lyme Regis, 23 July 1949. The small running shed which housed the one engine kept on the branch can be seen in the background. This interesting line, opened to traffic in 1903, was closed in November 1965.

[John H. Meredith]

Yeovil was served by a push-and-pull set which plied between the Town station and the Junction, almost two miles away on the West of England main line. The faithful 'M7s' provided power here for many years; No. 30129, built in 1911, propels the set towards the Junction on 24 July 1961.

[M. J. Fox]

No. 30129 at the platform in Yeovil Town station on 5 May 1957.   [A. E. Bennett]

The driver of No. 34091 *Weymouth* takes a breath of air as he works the 3.50 p.m. Yeovil to Waterloo out to the Junction, where the Pacific will run around the stock before setting off to London, 23 June 1963.　　　　[G. D. King]

Freight trains meet near Templecombe on 4 November 1961. The fireman of Maunsell 'S15' No. 30831 watches while his colleagues fight for adhesion as 'West Country' No. 34092 *City of Wells* restarts a freight from Salisbury. The robust construction of the splendid Maunsell 4-6-0 is evident in this view. The 5ft 7in driving wheels, long travel piston valves and a free steaming boiler made the class excellent mixed traffic engines.   [G. A. Richardson]

Maunsell's smaller mixed traffic design of 'N' Class 2-6-0s handled a wide variety of duties throughout the Southern system. No.31842 climbs towards Buckhorn Weston Tunnel, near Gillingham, with the 8.55 a.m. Ilfracombe to Salisbury, 4 November 1961.

[G. A. Richardson]

Salisbury has rostered the powerful rebuilt 'West Country' Pacific No. 34108 *Wincanton* for the humble but useful duty of a pick-up freight turn to Exmouth Junction yard, 30 May 1964. The engine, after shunting at Gillingham, the small Dorset town 105 miles from Waterloo, is coupling up to a horse box before proceeding on its way.   [J. R. Besley]

Another fine study of an 'S15' hard at work. The fireman adjusts the injectors as No. 30845 of Exmouth Junction (72A) shed labours up the gradient towards Semley with a Salisbury freight.

[G. A. Richardson]

The driver of rebuilt 'West Country' No.34025 *Whimple* has shut off for the curve at Chilmark as an up holiday relief rolls through the Wiltshire farmland on a summer Saturday in 1963.

[G. A. Richardson]

Evening sun lights up the grime on the paintwork of 'Merchant Navy' Pacific No.35026 *Lamport and Holt Line* as it reduces speed for the sharp curves at Wilton, three miles from the next stop at Salisbury, on 3 August 1964. The lines in the background are the ex-GWR tracks from Westbury, a route which carries freight and passenger traffic from Bristol and South Wales to southern England.

[M. Mensing]

Black smoke testifies to the hard work of the fireman as No.35030 *Elder Dempster Lines* hammers westwards near Tisbury with the 'Atlantic Coast Express' on 8 June 1963.   [G. A. Richardson]

The 1.0 p.m. from Waterloo eases towards the water column at the western end of Salisbury Number 4 platform behind No. 34052 *Lord Dowding* on 6 April 1964.

[Alan Wills]

Stopping trains for the West usually waited in the down bay (Number 5 platform) at Salisbury. No. 34091 *Weymouth* has steam up for its all-stations run to Exeter on 26 August 1962.

[K. A. Stone]

emanning the 'A.C.E.' at Salisbury on 7 April 1964. The Salisbury driver—having worked No. 35028 *Clan Line* non-stop
om Waterloo in 80 minutes for the 83 miles—gives the motion some quick attention with the oil-can as his fireman
mbs up the front step to the smoke box. The relieving Exmouth Junction driver opens the flow of water after his
eman has put the pipe in the water tank, while the Locomotive Inspector for the district discusses a point with
other official. Note the black metal box favoured by old Southern enginemen for carrying their personal belongings
the footplate. The 'W' on the post acts as a marker enabling the driver to make an accurate stop for water.

[Alan Wills]

A 'U' Class 2-6-0, No.31805, rebuilt by Maunsell from his 2-6-4T 'K' Class, coasts into Salisbury with a stopping train from Exeter on 7 August 1961. The signal box on the right, Salisbury C, is the ex-GWR box which controlled the Western goods yard and the GW route out of Salisbury. On the left is Salisbury West, a very busy box which controlled the western approaches to the station, the West goods yard as well as the movement of locomotives to and from the depot which is just visible in the distance.

[K. A. Stone]

Smoke, steam and thunderous noise at the east end of Salisbury station as the driver of No. 34003 *Plymouth* leaves with an up afternoon express for London on 23 October 1963. The start for up trains at Salisbury was one of the most difficult in the West Country, demanding enginemanship of the highest order from the drivers. The metals, laid on a rising gradient to a 10-chain reverse curve were usually liberally covered with oil which had escaped from Bulleid oil-baths, so the light-footed Pacifics tested the skill of the most experienced men. The stiff pull-out regulator handle required the most delicate operation to avoid spectacular slipping.   [K. A. Stone]

Bulleid 'Battle of Britain' light Pacific No. 34069 *Hawkinge*, piloting 'N' 2-6-0 No. 31833 on a down Ilfracombe train, approaches Yeoford, near the junction for the North Devon line, 16 August 1958. The single disc below the chimney was the route indication for this line.

[A. E. Bennett]

The steepness of the descent from Exeter (Central) to St. David's is clearly visible as this Portsmouth to Ilfracombe express, headed by 4-6-2 No. 34061 *73 Squadron*, with E1/R No. 32695 working back to the lower level as pilot, gathers momentum down the 1 in 37 gradient on 22 July 1955. This severe incline presented a considerable operating bottleneck, as most trains required assistance up the bank, while paths had to be found for the banking engines to return to St. David's for their next stint of work. The ten fifty-ton E1/Rs were Maunsell 1927 rebuilds of Stroudley's E1 0-6-0 tanks of 1874 vintage, with a radial trailing axle and a large coal bunker.

[Stanley Creer]

No. 31842 rolls past the wooden station buildings at Yeoford, eleven miles out from Exeter (Central). The train, the 2.10 p.m. from Ilfracombe, was typical of many West Country workings as it also had a coach from the 2.7 p.m. ex-Torrington which was combined with the 2.33 p.m. from Plymouth to form the 4.30 p.m. from Exeter to London.   [J. R. Besley]

The 5.15 p.m. Exeter to Barnstaple Junction scurries along in the evening sunlight towards Copplestone, the first station out from Yeoford along the North Devon line, with No.31840 in charge, 9 June 1963. [J. R. Besley]

The kind of scene which Dr. Beeching banished from the railways. No.31821, having shunted the yard and picked up three milk tanks from the Express Dairies Yeo Vale Creamery, steams past the outstretched arm of the signalman at Lapford with the 1.10 p.m. Barnstaple Junction to Exmouth Junction freight on 5 June 1964. [J. R. Besley]

Late afternoon at Eggesford, 5 June 1964. No. 34083 *605 Squadron* has come off the 3.25 p.m. Barnstaple Junction to Feltham freight, taking some of its load into the old cattle-dock siding to clear the single line for a passenger train. The crossing loop, like many on this line, is too short for a reasonably sized freight train. [J. R. Besley]

Pacific No. 34109 *Sir Trafford Leigh-Mallory* scatters the local hens as it approaches Eggesford, twenty miles from Exeter, on 16 August 1958. [A. E. Bennett]

No. 34015 *Exmouth* runs into Portsmouth Arms, the small country station 200¾ miles from Waterloo, on 16 August 1958, while a down train waits in the crossing loop.   [A. E. Bennett]

A general view of Portsmouth Arms on 4 June 1964, with No. 34107 *Blandford Forum* heading the 4.21 p.m. from Exeter Central to Ilfracombe and Torrington.   [J. R. Besley]

Passing the coal stage, delapidated Mogul No.31821 trundles the 1.10 p.m. pick-up goods away from Barnstaple Junction, 5 June 1964. The engine will shunt the sidings at all the stations along the line to Yeoford—a tedious, but once useful, task. [J. R. Besley]

A 'Battle of Britain' Pacific wends its way homeward to Exmouth Junction on a glorious summer day in August 1961; No.34078 *222 Squadron* at Barnstaple Junction with a general freight.
[D. T. Cobbe]

A 'stopper' from Exeter to Ilfracombe, with ex-LSWR stock next to the tender of 'West Country' 4-6-2 No. 34022 *Exmoor*, coasting into Mortehoe and Woolacombe in September 1953. This bleak, windswept station is at the summit of the long climb, partly at 1 in 40, from Braunton, six miles back along the line.   [J. R. Besley]

An Ilfracombe to Exeter train, hauled by No.34057 *Biggin Hill*, storms up the 1 in 36 bank to Mortehoe summit. This climb, one of the most gruelling in the West of England, necessitated a great deal of assistance for the heavier trains, but the Bulleid Pacific is making good progress with its five-coach load on 16 July 1955.

[Stanley Creer]

Having laboured up the long stretch of 1 in 40, 'N' Class Mogul No.31838 runs up the easier 1 in 330 incline into Mortehoe and Woolacombe in September 1959. These sure-footed 2-6-0s were extremely successful as freight engines over heavily graded lines on the Southern system.   [Derek Cross]

An 'M7' tank eases a local freight over the Taw Viaduct at Barnstaple, 18 July
949.   [John H. Meredith]

Modern motive power for a Torrington line freight. Bulleid Pacific No. 34106 *Lydford* rolls along the easy grades beside the River Torridge near Instow with the 12.45 p.m. Torrington to Barnstaple Junction. Some of the vans are through traffic for Feltham and beyond.

[J. R. Besley]

The Instow signalman holds out the tablet to the fireman of No. 41214, an Ivatt 2-6-2 tank working the Torrington to Barnstaple goods on 4 June 1964.

[J. R. Besley]

Ivatt 2-6-2T No. 41313 at Torrington with the one-coach 10.52 a.m. (S.O.) train from Halwill, 8 July 1961.

[J. R. Besley]

Ivatt tank No. 41290, of Barnstaple shed, pauses at Bideford with the Barnstaple to Torrington local as numerous boys leave the train for their nearby school at the beginning of term. These fine little tanks replaced the ageing Drummond 'M7s' in North Devon during the late 1950's. Designed for post-war conditions, easy access and maintenance were paramount considerations and the result produced by the LMS design staff proved most popular on the Southern Region.

[E. D. Burt]

Activity in the bright summer sunshine at Torrington; the fireman of No. 41283 takes water after the 14 mile trip from Barnstaple as No. 41290 waits with a single coach which will form the 3.55 p.m. to Halwill, 26 August 1964.   [P. J. Lynch]

Road and rail meet at Meeth. No. 41294 hauls the one coach forming the 10.38 a.m. from Halwill to Torrington on 8 April 1961.   [J. R. Besley]

Hatherleigh on 26 August 1964, with No.41290 on the 3.55 p.m. Torrington to Halwill. This little station could be taken as typical of those lonely rural retreats which saw few passengers and fewer trains, yet were so much part of the English country scene.   [P. J. Lynch]

Petrockstow, eight miles out from Torrington on the twenty mile run to Halwill, with 2-6-2T No.41297 at the head of a mixed train on 9 July 1962.
[H. C. Casserley]

The 'Exmoor Ranger' enthusiasts' special at Hole on 27 March 1965; spring sunshine glints on the polished black paintwork of Nos. 41291 and 41206.

[M. J. Fox]

An E1/R 0-6-2T No. 2610 in Southern Railway days at Hole, $2\frac{3}{4}$ miles from Halwill. The railway from Bideford reached Torrington in 1872, but the remaining section of the line was not completed until July 1925, when the Torrington to Halwill line, under the guise of the North Devon & Cornwall Junction Light Railway, was brought into operation, the last line of any length to be constructed in the West Country. The passenger trains were withdrawn in March 1965.

[Lens of Sutton]

No. 80039 does some
shunting with the stock
of the 12.04 p.m. from
Bude after arrival at
Halwill, 26 September
1964. The Standard '4s'
were popular performers
on the Bude line in the
final steam years.

[W. L. Underhay]

Looking down the line at
Halwill, 19 July 1949. E1/R No.
32095 stands in the bay with the
train from Torrington, as No.
34007 *Wadebridge* swings over
the points with the up
'Atlantic Coast Express' from
Padstow. In the background,
'M7' No. 30124 is ready to back
on with the through coach from
Bude.   [John H. Meredith]

The North Cornwall portion of the up 'A.C.E.' is headed into Crediton, seven miles west of Exeter Central, by 'West Country' Pacific No. 34035 *Shaftesbury* on 23 March 1963. The number 550 in the foreground refers to the bridge; the Southern numbered its bridges with this standard style of number plate for easy identification.   [J. R. Besley]

No. 31875 in Okehampton station with a six-coach North Cornwall line train, three vehicles for Padstow and the rear three for Bude, 17 August 1963. Many of these 'N' Class 2-6-0s were erected in Woolwich Arsenal after the Great War, and were thereafter always known to the men as 'Woolworths'.   [J. R. Besley]

'N' Class No.31843 shunts empty stock for a Padstow train at Okehampton on 27 April 1963. This station, situated high above the town, witnessed a great deal of dividing and joining of trains, as the Plymouth and North Cornwall lines parted company some three miles to the west at Meldon.

[W. L. Underhay]

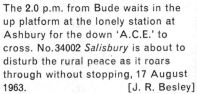

The 2.0 p.m. from Bude waits in the up platform at the lonely station at Ashbury for the down 'A.C.E.' to cross. No.34002 *Salisbury* is about to disturb the rural peace as it roars through without stopping, 17 August 1963.

[J. R. Besley]

'Battle of Britain' Pacific No.34076 *41 Squadron* at the head of the down 'Atlantic Coast Express' at Halwill on 9 July 1964. The advent of the Bulleid light Pacifics to this route in 1947 provided the line with modern machines for the through trains. These were often lightly loaded but at times even these powerful engines were taxed on the heavy grades when additional coaches were required to carry the large numbers of holiday-makers who used the line in the summer months before the Beeching era.

[D. T. Cobbe]

'N' Class No.31853 simmers quietly in the sun at Halwill on 26 August 1964, a few days before its withdrawal fro service. This engine, like many others of the class, ended its days with a Standard type chimney, which somewh altered its appearance.

[P. J. Lync

50

The station nameboard says it all—Halwill, the village whose importance was made by the coming of the railway and which has since slipped back into obscurity again. Quiet for long periods during the day, the station would suddenly burst into activity as trains on the Bude, Padstow and Torrington lines converged for a brief meeting. Here, the fireman on No. 31849 from Okehampton has just taken the tablet from the signalman, 9 June 1962. [J. R. Besley]

The 1.15 p.m. Bude to Exmouth Junction freight passes through Whitstone, and Bridgerule, five miles or so out from Bude, on 9 July 1964. The engine is carrying an 83D shedplate, the code long associated with Laira, but used by Exmouth Junction following its absorption by the WR in 1963.

[D. T. Cobbe]

Bude terminus, 18 August 1958, showing old favourite No. 30712, a 'T9' 4-4-0, built by Dubs of Glasgow in 1899. The line to Bude was closed to all traffic in October 1966.

[A. E. Bennett]

'Woolworth' No. 31844, having marshalled the 2.30 p.m. Okehampton goods, prepares to leave Bude yard, 17 August 1963. [J. R. Besley]

'N' Class 2-6-0 No. 31859 looks out of the small engine shed at Bude, 7 July 1964. Usually one tank engine was stabled overnight to work the early passenger turn on this branch, while visiting engines from Exmouth Junction were also serviced. The A.W.S. apparatus is prominent between the leading wheels of the locomotive, although these tracks were never equipped with the signalling system.

[D. T. Cobbe]

The North Cornwall line diverged from the Plymouth tracks at Meldon Junction, three miles west of Okehampton, but the Duchy was not actually entered until the crossing of the River Tamar just east of Launceston. The Devonshire station of Ashwater is depicted above, showing the 'Atlantic Coast Express' drifting through behind No.34031 *Torrington*, while veteran 'T9' 4-4-0 No. 30710 waits for the line to clear before continuing its journey up the long five mile pull to Halwill on 20 August 1958. The plume of steam at the dome-mounted safety valves shows that the fireman has built up the full boiler pressure of 175lbs per sq.in., ready for the effort ahead.

[A. E. Bennett]

Launceston, 'Gateway to Cornwall', with No.30710 at the head of an up passenger to Exeter, 20 August 1958. The West of England 'T 9s' were allocated to Exmouth Junction shed and were popular with their crews until the end of their service, being extremely reliable machines.

[A. E. Bennett]

The fireman on No.31818 receives the tablet as the 9.56 a.m. Okehampton to Padstow clatters into Launceston, 16 May 1963. The signal box is an interesting double-sided structure, the rear half serving the Western Region lines hidden in the background. [J. R. Besley]

In September 1959, the 'T9s' were still performing daily on the North Cornwall line. No.30715, built in 1899 by Dubs of Glasgow—for £2,945—was superheated in 1924 and remained in active service until 1961, a good investment by any standards. She is seen leaving Otterham with the 'Perisher', the 3.13 p.m. from Padstow.

[Derek Cross]

Camelford station, 1¼ miles from the town and 800ft above sea level, is shrouded in the Atlantic mists which often sweep in from the nearby coast; No.31818 steams away past the box on 16 May 1963.

[J. R. Besley]

'Battle of Britain' Pacific No. 34079 *141 Squadron*, with pre-war coaches in tow, makes the easy down-hill start away from Delabole with an up morning passenger in August 1962. To the left of the line is the mammoth Delabole Quarry, world famous for the quality of its slate. The quarry railway system was originally of 3ft gauge, but later converted to 1ft 11in, locomotives being first introduced in 1879. With the coming of the North Cornwall line, the slate was then despatched from Delabole station.

[G. D. King]

A featherweight load for Pacific No.34004 *Yeovil* as she climbs the 1 in 73 bank eastwards out of St. Kew Highway towards Port Isaac Road in 1953. Having worked down with the 'Atlantic Coast Express' the previous day, the engine has stabled overnight at Wadebridge. It worked the handful of wagons forming the 7.20 a.m. goods to Padstow, from thence home to Exeter with the 8.30 a.m. up 'A.C.E.', manned by Wadebridge men as far as Launceston.

[Brian A. Butt]

The Okehampton driver of 'N' 2-6-0 No.31840 peers ahead up the bank towards St. Kew Highway as his train, the 12.58 p.m. from Padstow, leaves the wooded Camel valley, 25 August 1962.

[G. D. King]

Morning activity at Wadebridge, September 1959. The driver of No.31846 has opened the regulator to recover from the severe slowing past Wadebridge East box and steams up to the platform with the 'Paper Train' which departed from Waterloo at 1.25 a.m., conveying a few passengers and many thousands of newspapers to West Country towns. While the papers are unloaded the ancient station pilot, Beattie well tank No.30586, detaches a van. This tank, built in 1875, one of three survivors of a design dating from 1863, was usually retained at Wadebridge as pilot and occasionally worked down to Padstow on passenger turns when there had been an engine failure.

[Derek Cross]

'Through train to London!' The 'Atlantic Coast Express' gave North Cornwall a good through service to the Capital for many years, but—alas—no more. The final run of this famous train was in September 1964 and the complete closure of the North Cornwall line in October 1966 left vast tracts of rural Cornwall and Devon without through public transport to the rest of Britain. In September 1959, however, the 'A.C.E.' is well patronised as it leaves Wadebridge behind No. 34058 *Sir Frederick Pile*.

[Derek Cross]

'T9' No.30717, a regular in Cornwall, runs into Wadebridge with the 10.55 a.m. from Padstow on 18 March 1961. The engine's roster comprised three trips between Padstow and Wadebridge, before departing home to Exeter with the 6.0 p.m. from Padstow (the 'Mail'). [Alan Wills]

The morning goods to Exmouth Junction waits for departure time in Wadebridge yard, 12 June 1964, powered by 'N' No.31406. The other Mogul on shed will work the 4.40 p.m. goods to Exmouth Junction after a trip to Bodmin in the afternoon. The barrels by the shed contain lubricating oil for locomotives using the depot. [Alan Wills]

Inside the wooden shed building, two more of Wadebridge's tanks, Beattie No.30587 and Adam
'O2' 0-4-4T No.30200 rest quietly between duties, 10 May 1958.   [Brian Morrison]

Wadebridge shed (72F) was situated some 85 miles from its parent depot, Exmouth Junction, so the shed fitters had to tackle as much repair work as possible with the limited equipment available at such a small establishment. As Beattie No.30585 weighed only a modest 38 tons, the use of jack and packing enabled the wheels to be dropped for attention to the axle boxes. Fortunately this little engine has been preserved and can now be seen at Quainton Road, near Aylesbury.   [Brian Morrison]

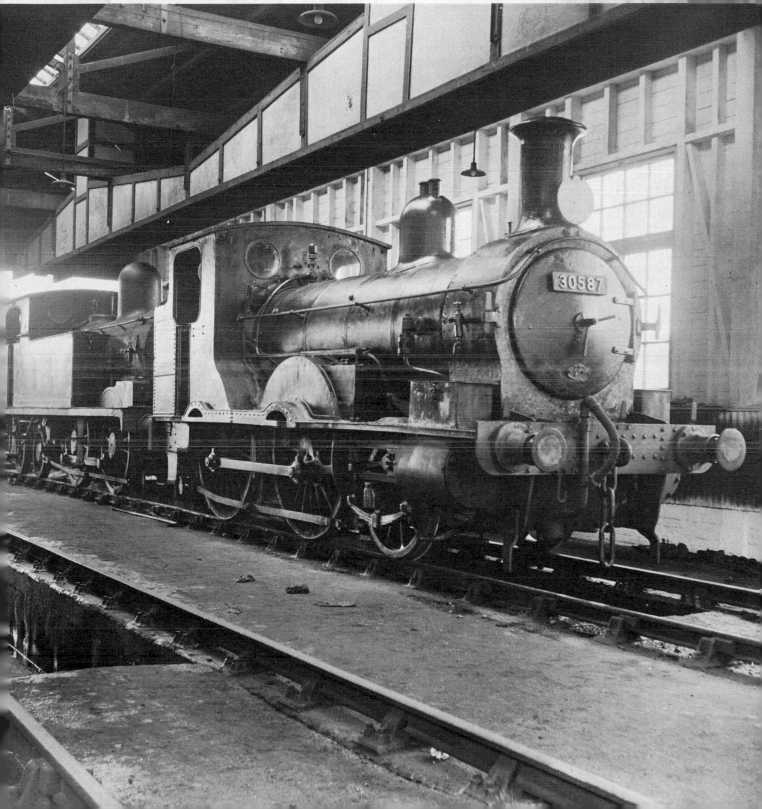

The 8.48 a.m. to Exeter (Central) prepares to leave Padstow behind Mogul No.31846 on 2 July 1964. This was the westernmost outpost of the old L S W R system, 259 miles from Waterloo. The metals reached this small Cornish port in 1899 and the final train exploded the traditional farewell detonators on 28 January 1967.   [D. T. Cobbe]

The west-bound 'A.C.E.' near the end of its journey crossing the Iron Bridge over Little Petherick Creek, just short of the Padstow terminus, 17 May 1962. The driver of No.34033 *Chard* has eased his mount down to 15mph in order to observe the severe speed restriction over the viaduct. The heavier rebuilt Bulleid Pacifics were banned from crossing this structure so they never operated on the North Cornwall route. The viaduct is still in place, but the lines were removed in 1967, marking the end of one of the most picturesque stretches of railway in Britain.   [D. T. Cobbe]

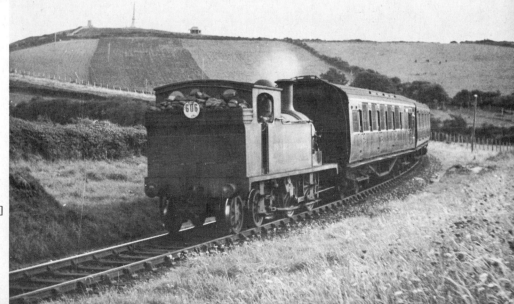

A local train from Bodmin
North approaches Padstow
behind No.30193 on 19 August
1950.   [L.&G.R.P.]

The ex-LSWR station, Bodmin North, on 19 August 1958 with 'Woolworth' No.31842, with steam up ready to run tender first to Wadebridge with an afternoon local. The branch service was withdrawn in January 1967.   [A. E. Bennett]

The final steam power for the Bodmin branch trains were the Ivatt Class '2' 2-6-2 tanks. The Adams 'O2s' were replaced by ex-GWR 0-6-0 pannier tanks in 1960, but although strong pullers, they were not popular with the SR crews on account of their poor riding qualities, but the Ivatts met with general approval. No. 41272 swings away from Wadebridge towards Bodmin in August 1962. [G. D. King]

'Woolworth' No. 31860 works the 12.25 p.m. Wadebridge to Bodmin North on 17 May 1962. Although Moguls were rostered to work the daily freight turn, they seldom appeared on passenger trains to Bodmin. This sylvan setting is near Dunmere Halt, with the 2-6-0 tackling the 1 in 48 up to the terminus at Bodmin. [D. T. Cobbe]

The three Beattie well tanks were among the most photographed engines in Britain. Built 1874–5, the three survivors were at Wadebridge by the turn of the century and were used on the sharply curved Wenford line, hauling a daily load of clay from the Stannon clay works, situated near the Wenford end of the line. Following extensive repairs in 1931, the trio survived until 1962, when '1366' Class 0-6-0PTs from the Western Region proved highly competent substitutes. This view, taken on 16 August 1961, shows No. 30585 shunting the clay sidings at Stannon.

[D. T. Cobbe]

No.30585 again, forging steadily ahead through Helland Woods, a beautiful section on the Wenford line, in September 1959. The 9.35 a.m. goods to Wenford was the prerogative of the senior driver at Wadebridge, who proudly kept his engine in splendid condition.

[Derek Cross]

The replacement; Collett tank No.1369 was the regular engine on the Wenford turn for two years until replaced by a diesel in 1964.

Another banker at Exeter; 'W' Class 2-6-4T No. 31916, having spent most of her life working inter-regional transfer freights in the London area, moved first to Eastleigh (note the 71A shedplate) and now has arrived at Exmouth Junction to help on the bank, 5 December 1962.   [J. R. Besley]

n up freight comes to rest in Exeter (Central), having made the climb up from St. David's behind Maunsell 'N' Class 2-6-0, with 'Z' 0-8-0T No. 30952 as pilot, September 1961.   [G. D. King]

For several years 'Z' Class 0-8-0T No. 30956 shunted in Exmouth Junction marshalling yard, but following the dieselisation of that duty, the engine was used as a powerful replacement for the ageing E1/Rs on the banking turns between St. David's and Central stations. The crew make good use of a quiet moment at Central, 13 August 1962. The fireman tops up the 1,500 gallon water supply, while the driver oils the Walschaerts valve gear. The three wisps of steam from the cylinder cocks reveal that this is a three cylinder engine, an unusual feature for a shunter, but one which made for smooth application of power at low speeds.

[J. R. Besley]

The Plymouth, Padstow and Bude portions of the down 'A.C.E.' made up a substantial load on 30 August 1957, resulting in the operating authorities working the train with two Pacifics to Okehampton; No.34025 *Whimple* pilots No.34060 *25 Squadron* as the train pulls out of St. David's under the typical GWR signal gantry.

[G. D. King]

A reminder of Southern Railway days at Exeter. No.21C112 *Launceston* was only a few months old on 26 August 1946 when seen at Cowley Bridge Junction, working a train of rather ancient stock. The engine is in its original condition and several features to note include the circular 'Southern' smokebox plate, short smoke deflectors and narrow cab spectacles. The unrebuilt Bulleids, both 'M.N.' and 'W.C.', looked much more distinguished in their bright and cheerful malachite green livery, contrasting with the Brunswick green of BR days which—whisper it not in Swindon!—seemed drab by comparison.

[Brian A. Butt]

Next stop St. David's for 'N' Class No.31839 as it eases away from Newton St. Cyres on the 11.48 a.m. Plymouth to Exeter, 28 July 1962. The neat proportions of the engine and tender show to advantage in this rear view.　　　　　[J. R. Besley]

Mogul No.31835, carrying the Plymouth to Waterloo headcode, hurries towards Yeoford on 28 July 1962 with the combined 1.5 p.m. ex-Padstow and the 2.33 p.m. ex-Plymouth.　　　　　[J. R. Besley]

Grimy 'Woolworth' No.31846 pulls slowly out of Yeoford with an up ballast train on 23 March 1963. A great quantity of stone was carried from the Southern's own quarry at Meldon to all parts of the Region.　　　　[W. L. Underhay]

A long rake of wagons snakes out of Okehampton yard at 12.15 p.m. on 9 June 1962, bound for Exmouth Junction behind No.31843.

[J. R. Besley]

No.34030 *Watersmeet* leaves Yeoford with a Plymouth train, July 1951. The electric headlamps, operated by a steam turbo-generator, are prominent on the front of the locomotive. Electric lights also illuminated the wheels, motion and cab fittings, a popular feature of the Bulleid Pacifics.

[Derek Cross]

USA tank No. DS234 (ex-No. 30062) was the only steam locomotive at work on BR metals west of Exeter when this photograph was taken at Meldon Quarry on 29 October 1965. The 'Yankie' engines, purchased from the US Army Transportation Corps after the Second World War, were popular with the SR enginemen, first in Southampton Docks and later at various Service Depots.

[J. R. Besley]

No. 34023 *Blackmore Vale* storms away from Okehampton with a Brighton to Plymouth train, July 1964. The driver is using the steam sanders to gain adhesion, the Bulleids being notorious for slipping. The high power-to-weight ratio was one contributory factor, but this was aggravated by oil from the oil bath, which enclosed the chain-driven valve gear, reaching the rails beneath the driving wheels.   [D. T. Cobbe]

Back in Southern Railway days, 2-6-0 No. 1856 rumbles across Meldon Viaduct over the gorge of the West Okement River with a down train, 27 August 1945. The extensive Meldon quarry workings are visible in the background.   [H. C. Casserley]

Apart from the BR livery of 'M7' No. 30037, this scene near Bere Alston could well be 1914 instead of 1954. LSWR stock and loco-motive look very much at home in this setting on the edge of Dartmoor as they form the local train running between Tavistock and Plymouth.

[Brian A. Butt]

No. 30037 again, among the shrubs in lonely Brentor station 28 June 1956.

[J. H. Aston]

Unkempt and neglected in appearance, yet still capable of useful service, another of Exmouth Junction's hardworking Moguls, No. 31845, shunts the 12.44 p.m. Friary to Exmouth Junction freight in Bere Alston yard on 15 September 1962. The Meldon Junction to Bere Alston section of this once-important main line was closed to all traffic in May 1968.   [J. R. Besley]

The Callington branch train stands in Bere Alston station with Ivatt No. 41295 at its head.
[Lens of Sutton]

With a white plume of steam from the safety valves contrasting with the cloudy sky above Dartmoor, 4-6-2 No. 34036 *Westward Ho* speeds down the line between Lydford and Tavistock with the 9.0 a,m, from Waterloo on 27 September 1957. Western Region's Mary Tavy station, on the Plymouth to Launceston line, can be seen on the extreme left.

[W. L. Underhay]

The 10.2 a.m. ex-Plymouth portion of the up 'A.C.E.' leaving Tavistock (North) behind Mogul No. 31844 on the last day of March 1962. All the 'N' Class 2-6-0s in the West were concentrated at Exmouth Junction shed which, at that date, still had 25 of these stalwarts on its strength.

[J. R. Besley]

On 16 August 1958, 'O2' No.30193 of Plymouth Friary shed takes water at Callington branch, originally a narrow gauge mineral line, which was developed by the P D S W J R from
1900. This 0-4-4 tank, built to the designs of William Adams in 1890, has had its original boiler
replaced by one of Drummond pattern, recognisable by the safety valves mounted on the dome.
The engine remained in service until April 1962.   [A. E. Bennett]

...o. 30193 halted beside the ...mple wooden station building ...Gunnislake, 4½ miles along ...e branch from Bere Alston.
[A. E. Bennett]

...e train pauses at Latchley, ...o miles further on.
[A. E. Bennett]

Lonely Luckett, windswept and bleak, provided few passengers for the branch trains which plied through this rural area.   [A. E. Bennett]

Journey's end. No. 30193 has arrived at Callington and reverses before the fireman unhooks from the L S W R coaches.   [A. E. Bennett]

On 15 August 1956, the branch traffic was in the hands of 'O 2', No. 30225, which is running round its train. The engine shed is on the left.

[Hugh Davies]

The terminus at Callington, 15 September 1962, with the 1.0 p.m. to Bere Alston standing under the station roof, with modern motive power at its head. Ivatt tank No. 41216, originally built for the LMS, finishes its days far from home in this West Country setting. The Gunnislake to Callington section of the branch was closed in November 1966.

[J. R. Besley]

The 'O2s' were useful little tanks for light branch duties, and a number were shedded at Plymouth (Friary) for local passenger turns and such freight trips as this pick-up goods from Keyham, seen at Devonport (King's Road) on 18 August 1961. This station was the first LSWR terminus in the Plymouth district, opened on 18 May 1876. When the Lydford–Devonport section of line was opened in 1890, LSWR trains ran through to North Road station, and this terminus was turned into a through station.

[D. T. Cobbe]

It could be argued that the 'M7' 0-4-4 tanks were Drummond's best LSWR design, for even the mighty 'T9s' had to be superheated before they gave of their best. But the 'M7s' were little altered during their sixty odd years reign, the final example lasting until 1964. No. 30034 speeds a Plymouth to Tavistock North local along the favourable grades near Devonport (King's Road), 18 August 1961.

[D. T. Cobbe]

Southern Region trains ran through the Western Region station at North Road (now called simply Plymouth) on their way to and from the S R terminus at Friary. However, No. 34058 *Sir Frederick Pile* has been at work on a Western train running from Exeter via Newton Abbot. The 'clues' are the W R stock and the standard British headcode for a slow passenger train instead of the S R disc route indication. After the long downhill run from Hemerdon, the boiler pressure has built up and the safety valves are about to lift with a shattering roar.   [Brian A. Butt]

An interior view of Friary shed, 10 May 1958. Nos. 30088 and 30089 are part of the shed's allocation of the small but useful 'B4' dock tanks. These little Adams tanks were built at Nine Elms in 1892 and were used at various restricted locations throughout the system. The spark arrestors fitted to the Friary tanks enabled the engines to work near the timber yards at Oreston.

[Brian Morrison]

The Southern terminus at Friary was opened by the LSWR in 1891. Trains from it ran through North Road (in the down direction) to reach Exeter and Waterloo, while local services operated to St. Budeaux, Turnchapel and Tavistock. No. 34109 *Sir Trafford Leigh-Mallory* departs with a London train on 20 August 1958, while WR 2-6-0 No. 7333 waits to follow with a slow to Exeter via Okehampton, a balancing working to that noted on page 90. The last train from the terminus ran on Sunday, 14 September 1958.

[A. E. Bennett]

No. 30757 *Earl of Mount Edgcumbe* and No. 30758 *Lord St. Levan* were built by Hawthorn Leslie for the PDSWJR in 1907. They are seen, with 'M7' No. 30037, at Friary on 20 August 1954.   [R. M. Casserley]

93

The Southern and Great Western men at Exeter and Plymouth worked turns over each others tracks in order to gain additional route knowledge to cope with emergencies. Thus we have the spectacle of Southern engines in settings made famous in countless photographs of Western trains in action. The chattering Lemaitre exhaust of No. 21C112 *Launceston* makes an alien sound as she pounds up Dainton towards the tunnel on 30 September 1946.

[Brian A. Butt]

Southern Steam on the sea-wall at Dawlish Warren, 26 September 1946. 'West Country' Pacific No.21C113, soon to be named *Okehampton* heads for Exeter and home with a stopping passenger train.   [Brian A. Butt]

'N' Class No. 1833, steaming well, dashes past Aller Junction to make a flying start at the climb up Dainton bank in September 1946. The Nationalised authorities continued to operate these inter-Regional turns throughout the steam era.

[Brian A. Butt]

No apology need be made for yet one more view of the 'Atlantic Coast Express'. This is the last run of this famous train, seen swooping out of Buckhorn Weston Tunnel on 5 September 1964 behind 'Merchant Navy' No. 35022 *Holland America Line*, of Nine Elms shed, with her Exmouth Junction driver peering ahead towards Templecombe. The 'A.C.E.' with its through carriages to so many distant destinations, was the epitome of Southern service to the West Country and with its ending, the status of the Region declined immediately. Now the Salisbury to Exeter line is very much a poor relation, with a shadow hanging over its future existence.

[Norman E. Preedy]